REAL ESTATE AS AN INVESTMENT
WORKING WITH INVESTORS

REAL ESTATE AS AN INVESTMENT
WORKING WITH INVESTORS

by
Tom Whitehouse CRB,CRS,GRI

Copyright © 2020 by Tom Whitehouse
All rights reserved. No part of this book may be reproduced, scanned,
or distributed in any printed or electronic form without permission.
First Edition: November, 2020
Printed in the United States of Ameri
ISBN: 978-1-648-58773-3

To Ruthie, my biggest supporter. She always believed in me.

Table of Contents

Part One: Fundamentals of Investment Real Estate

1. Assemble Your Team
2. Determine Your Objectives
3. Ownership Interest in Real Property
4. Protecting Your Assets
5. Four Financial Benefits
6. Mortgage or Pay Cash

Part Two: Valuing Investment Real Estate

7. Methods of Valuation
8. Capitalization Rate Explained
9. How Much Should I Pay For The Property

Part Three: Time To Move The Equity

10. Evaluating Your ROI
11. Time To Move The Equity

Part Four: 1031 Exchange

- 12. Tax Benefits of Exchanges
- 13. The Exchange Process
- 14. Other Exchange Considerations

Part Five: Tax Strategy For Investment RE

- 15. Reporting Income
- 16. Deductible Expenses
- 17. Depreciation of Rental Property
- 18. Reporting Income, Expenses And Losses

Part Six: Your IRA Can Own Real Estate

- 19. Self- Directed IRA
- 20. Rules For IRA Investment

Preface

I wrote this book to discuss the procedures and benefits of real estate investment and also to assist my fellow real estate professionals by providing the knowledge and tools that you need when working with investor clients.

This book is about wealth building. There is a big difference between wealth and income. We all know people who have an enormous income but never seem to have any money, big house big mortgage, big cars big car payments. But we also know that someday the income will end and what we will be left with is the wealth that we built over the years.

I'd like to share a story that goes way back to when I was young. My Father had a friend named Don, in fact our families were friends. Don's daughters were friends with my sisters so our families were often together. The one thing I remember well was that Don always talked about rental properties that he had purchased. Every time we saw him he would talk about the property he just purchased. They weren't expensive and always needed a lot of work so my dad would help out with painting and minor repairs.

Don went to work for the local Whirlpool factory right out of high school and worked there his entire career as a fork truck driver. He probably never made $10 an hour in his life. One day while I was in college, I went by to see my dad and he said guess what, Don retired. I said good for him and then Dad said do you remember those rental houses that he was always buying? Well he sold them and put a half million dollars in the bank. On his wages, Don could never have accumulated that much money, he had built wealth through real estate investments.

I have a business degree in accounting and spent 18 years working in corporate accounting. The last job I had before starting my real estate career, I was the CFO of a $350 million company in Ann Arbor MI involved in mergers and acquisitions. We were buying companies which often included real estate.

When I decided to change careers, I figured that I could use that knowledge to work with clients interested in real estate investing. In order to grow that business I started holding real estate investment seminars for the public. I would get a meeting room at the local Holiday Inn and since this was before the internet and social media, I would advertise in the papers and put up flyers at the banks and grocery stores in the area. I was having some success, 12-15 people attending the seminars, but I always thought there should be more.

That year in November, I attended the NAR convention and sat in on an investment class. After the class I met John from Illinois. He asked me if I was doing seminars and I told him I was. He asked if I was having success and I said "kind of". I told him I wasn't having the attendance that I thought I would. He then asked me how much I was charging. I told him, "no, it's free" and he said that's the problem. Then he said the public views free seminars in two ways. One, if it's free it must not be any good, or two, it's probably not really free. When I get there they will expect me to buy something. I've seen many real estate seminars that do exactly that. So I asked John how much he charged and he said $89.

When I got home I was planning my next seminar and I decided to charge $89. I advertised the same as always and I had 26 people attend my next seminar. I sold 8 of them property over the next 6 months. Not only did the number of attendees increase, they were also more serious about investing.

After reading this book there are three possible outcomes that could positively affect your real estate career.

1) You may decide to do your own investment seminars. You'll learn the process for producing successful real estate investments that you can share with the public and believe me, they want to know.

2) I hope this will inspire you to invest in real estate. I recently read a surprising statistic that only around 3% of licensed real estate agents own investment property. This is the business you're in, and you're in a perfect position to take advantage of it.

3) This information will help you when working with investor clients or other clients that you might encourage to become investors by sharing the benefits and potential ROI.

Real Estate As An Investment

Several years ago I got a call from Ron who lived in Boston. He told me he and his wife vacationed often in Florida and asked if I could help them find their own place. Of course I said yes. They flew down and I helped them buy a second home. About six months later Ron called and told me his friend Jim had stayed in their place and decided he wanted a place of his own and wondered if I could help Jim and his wife. Again, I said yes, they came down and I helped them buy a second home.

When they would visit we would often go out to dinner with our families and we all became friends. Jim and Ron both play golf so I often joined them for a round. One Saturday we had finished playing and were having lunch and I asked both of them if they had investments. They said they did, stocks, bonds etc. I asked if they ever considered investing in real estate. Both said no but asked if they should consider. I then proceeded to give my 15 minute presentation of the benefits and potential return on investment with real estate. When I finished they both said "I'm in". Over the next year Ron bought 4 properties and Jim bought 3 and both are interested in buying more. I encourage my clients to put some of their investment dollars in real estate and that it is actually safer than the stock market.

Think of this, could you buy a stock today and wake up tomorrow and the stock be worth zero? Of course, it has happened many times over the years. So then, could you buy real estate today and wake up tomorrow and it be worth zero? Very unlikely. It could go down in value but would not lose all of its value. I do also remind them that it is not as liquid as stocks so don't invest money that you might need in 30 days. It is a long term investment.

Let me tell you what this book is NOT about.

1) It's not a "get rich quick" scheme. I haven't figured out how to get rich quick in real estate, so if you do, please let me know. This is long term investing to build wealth.

2) It's not about how to "flip" houses. That is a legitimate strategy but not one that I cover here.

3) It's also not about "how to buy real estate with no money". There are plenty of those seminars and YouTube videos. We are talking about real investors with real money to invest.

I hope this information is helpful and adds another layer to your successful real estate career.

Most of the discussion and many of the examples in this book are centered around residential income property as opposed to commercial property. However, the formulas and analysis will work for both.

Tom Whitehouse

Introduction

So why **real estate as an investment**? The strong desire to accumulate wealth and generate a stream of income is certainly the primary reason for the substantial interest in owning real property in this country. Nearly everyone lists real estate ownership as one of their highest goals in life.

For investors, it provides a profitable way to diversify their portfolio and be able to shelter income through deductions of operating expenses, interest and depreciation.

Real estate is defined as the land and any permanent structures or improvements attached to the land, whether natural or man-made.

Owning real estate is not just the possession of the physical property but also includes certain legal rights to the continual peaceful utilization and redistribution. When we acquire real estate, we also acquire a **bundle of rights** for the property. The rights of use are, possession, control, enjoyment, exclusion and disposition, including the right to pass the property on by means of a will, and this changes the definition of real estate to **real property**.

A real estate investment can be described as the commitment of funds with a goal of preserving and increasing wealth and earning a profit. In some instances, investment also represents the forfeiture of some present comforts in anticipation of future benefits.

A real estate investment can often require things as important as money, it often involves the investment of personal time and effort known as **sweat equity**.

Being able to invest in real estate extends beyond our daily commitments. These funds that are in excess of our life's necessities, often known as **discretionary funds**, can be viewed as the money available for investment.

The advantages of real estate investments include the possibilities of high yield, and total control over the capital invested. As you will see in later chapters, the annual return on investment can be 25-30%.

There are also opportunities to leverage the investment. While most security investments, such as stocks and bonds, will allow you to borrow up to 50% of the value, you can often borrow 80% or more of the value of the real estate.

The disadvantages of real estate investment includes relatively poor liquidity. You never want to invest funds into real estate that you may need in the coming months. There is also the necessity of constant management, but keeping the property up to date and well maintained will also improve the value of the investment.

So here are some of the misconceptions about investing in real estate.

Investing in Real estate is Complicated.

Well, actually, it's only as complicated as you make it. It can be complicated, but you need to focus on the aspects that matter the most. When you do, you'll start to understand the fundamental things you need to know to be successful. Then you will see that it's probably simpler than you imagined. When you focus on things in the correct order, you will acquire the knowledge more quickly and easily.

Investing is Risky, I Could Lose Money.

The key is to follow sound investment principles and models to take the risk out of play. So investing isn't about taking risks, it is about having sound criteria, the patience to find the opportunities, and a willingness to take action quickly. Investing will not be completely risk free but having a plan will make it less risky.

Successful Investors Know The When to Invest.

One question that I often get from investor clients is, "Tom, is this a good time to invest in real estate?" My answer is always the same, **YES**. If you have a formula, which we will create in a later chapter, you simply find properties, plug them into the formula, if it works you buy it, if it doesn't you don't. There will always be properties that work in every market.

So **real estate as an investment**, as you'll see in the coming chapters, is a very good way to build wealth, income and create a valuable asset for your estate.

Tom Whitehouse

PART ONE

FUNDAMENTALS OF INVESTMENT REAL ESTATE

Tom Whitehouse

Chapter 1

Assemble Your Team

As you begin to work with investors, it is important to help them assemble the team of professionals that will work together to insure their success. The team includes:

1) **Real Estate Professional** – Once you have met with the investor, understand their goals and objectives, you will be in a position to save them time and make sure that the properties that they consider align with their goals and objectives.

2) **Mortgage Lender** – You will need to partner with a mortgage lender that understands investment real estate. Once they have the necessary information from

the investor they will have the ability to move quickly through the process. It is best to have a local lender to meet with that knows the market and is interested in becoming part of the team.

3) **Attorney** – Find a local real estate attorney that understands investment real estate, both residential and commercial. As with other real estate transactions, an attorney is not always required, but some of the transactions are more complicated and require some legal expertise.

4) **Accountant** – As with the other team members, it is important to find an accountant that understands investment real estate and the tax laws that apply. Often the tax benefits of the transaction will make or break the deal so their expertise will be an important part of the professional team.

This team of professionals providing knowledge of the market, financial, legal and accounting analysis, will lead your investors to create a successful investment portfolio.

Chapter 2

Determine Your Objectives

When working with investor clients, it is very important to determine and understand their goals and objectives. Some will be short term in nature and others long term but we need to know this in order to find properties that will meet their objectives.

Over the years I have discovered that most real estate investors' objectives fall into one of the following three categories.

1) Positive cash flow – Income. Many investors are looking for cash flow or are wanting to create an additional stream of income. Investors looking for positive cash flow will most often pay cash for the

property. This can certainly be accomplished with the right type of property. In this case the property operating cost would need to be substantially lower than the rental income. The type of property that often works for this objective would be a condo or other units in multi-unit structures. While you will be paying the condo association a monthly fee, it usually covers the building and structural maintenance.

Here is an example of a property recently purchased by one of my investors. The condo cost $145,000. The monthly condo fee was $350, taxes were $1200 per year and insurance was $1150 per year. Other repairs and maintenance averaged $1550 per year. The rental income was $1400 per month. So if you do the math:

Annual rental income	$15,800
Condo fee	- 4,200
Taxes and Insurance	- 2,350
Repairs and Maintenance	- 1,550
Cash flow before taxes	$ 7,700

This equates to a 5.3% cash return on investment, often referred to as "cash on cash". As you will see in later chapters, a cash on cash return of 5-7% is a good investment.

2) Long term ROI – Many investors are not interested in creating a stream of income but are focused on the long term return on their investment. Most often these investors will mortgage the property to reduce the cash invested. As long as the rental income covers their operating cost and interest on the mortgage, they will be focused on the long term return which will often be 20-30%

3) Tax Shelter – Many investors invest in real estate to create tax shelters to offset income from other sources. As you will see in later chapters, many times an income property will have a positive cash flow and yet show a loss for tax purposes. There are limits and other factors in the tax code that will affect the investors ability to take advantage of this opportunity, but with a good accountant and careful analysis this objective can often be met.

Tom Whitehouse

Chapter 3

Ownership Interest in Real Estate

How an investor holds title to real estate can have a significant impact on the degree of personal involvement in management and the amount of profit to be earned, taxes to be paid, and personal liability for debts and damages. In this chapter we will examine the forms of ownership interest in real property by individuals.

Individuals may acquire legal interest in real property, called **fee simple ownership**. An estate in fee simple implies that the owner has the greatest bundle of rights to the use of the property. Included in this bundle is the right to use, possess, finance, lease, inherit, and sell among others. Without partners to please or shareholders to impress, individuals may design their investment portfolio to meet their own immediate and long-term goals. Individual ownership of real estate demands that the investor take an active role in investment management.

Before we examine the forms of individual ownership, a distinction must be made concerning an individual owner's rights of property control. An owner can hold a fee simple title or an undivided interest subject to the right of inheritability or survivorship.

Inheritability implies that the control individuals have over their estates includes the right to designate who will inherit the property. These designations are described in the owner's will and require a legal probate procedure before the estate can be distributed to the heirs.

Survivorship on the other hand, eliminates this personal control over the distribution of the estate after death. When two or more persons enter into a survivorship form of ownership, they give up their individual rights and designate that on one owner's death, the other(s) in the agreement will be the recipient(s) of the deceased's portion of the property. The interest of the deceased pass automatically and immediately to the survivors.

The various forms of individual ownership include tenancy by the entirety, tenancy in common, community property, joint tenancy with rights of survivorship, sole and separate ownership, ownership in severalty, and dower and curtesy rights.

Tenancy by the Entirety

Tenancy by the Entirety is an arrangement limited to husbands and wives that includes the automatic right of survivorship and is not available in community property states. The owners are considered to be one entity, and when one spouse dies, the other becomes the immediate sole owner. Neither the husband or wife may unilaterally dispose of his or her interest.

Tenancy in Common

Recognized in all states, **tenancy in common** is an arrangement in which each of several participants controls and has an interest in an undivided portion of the entire property. The basic components of tenancy in common are the concepts of inheritability and undivided interest. Inheritability provides individual owners with the right to designate to whom their proportionate share of the property will pass on their death. Undivided interest implies that no single participant can identify his or her specific portion of the subject property, but rather had the rights to the entire property and its benefits as per his or her proportionate share.

Joint Tenancy with Rights of Survivorship

All but four states recognize **joint tenancy**, whereby participants, not necessarily husband and wife, own equal undivided interest in property, subject to the rights of survivorship. Any joint tenant may sell their interest, but the joint tenancy arrangement will be discontinued and the new owner will assume a role as a tenant in common with the remaining owners.

Community Property

With **community property**, which applies only to husbands and wives, monies earned during marriage and property purchased with these community funds belong equally to each spouse, who, simultaneously, maintains his or her inheritable rights. Thus, the community property spousal relationship is exactly opposite to the survivorship rights of spouses who are tenants by the entirety.

Sole and Separate Ownership

All states recognize **sole and separate ownership** of property, which is an inheritable estate. This form of ownership vests title to property in the name of one spouse while implying that the other is still alive but has signed over his or her interest. Sole and separate ownership can be utilized to take advantage of special property tax exemptions, to simplify property management, or to avoid inheritance taxes.

Severalty Ownership

All states acknowledge that single persons, whether unmarried or divorced, as well as widows and widowers, own their real property in **severalty**, also known as sole ownership. Severalty is an inheritable estate, because it is necessary to have two or more persons to establish a survivorship estate. Thus, owners in severalty should designate by will to whom they wish property to be distributed upon their death. Corporate ownership is a form of severalty.

Dower and Curtesy Rights

Finally, most states recognize the legal rights of a surviving spouse in the real estate of the deceased husband or wife. The rights of a widow in the property of her deceased husband are called **dower rights**, while the rights of a widower in the property of his deceased wife are called **curtesy rights**. The degree to which these rights are respected varies from state to state.

Chapter 4

Protecting Your Assets

Many real estate investors assume the most they have at risk in a failed real estate offer is their earnest money. Unfortunately, these false beliefs can result in thousands of dollars in damages to a seller if the deal does not close and the seller can prove their actual damages are more than the buyer's earnest money.

When making offers on investment real estate not financed by Freddie Mac or Fannie Mae, the protected real estate investor will make the offer and enter into a contract in the name of an LLC or Corporation. This protects the investor individually from potential claims if anything goes wrong with the deal.

Putting a property in your personal name takes all of the guesswork out of any attempted litigation down the road. This leaves you exposed to frivolous claims that could likely cost thousands of dollars in legal fees.

As a real estate investor you should not place multiple properties into the same LLC. Each one of those properties would become exposed to the risks and liabilities of the other properties. Avoid this risk by placing one property into each LLC. This will ensure that any liability associated with a property will stay contained in the one LLC and not risk other investments.

If you are financing the investment with conventional financing, you can transfer the property into the LLC after closing using a quitclaim deed. Only those on the mortgage should be members of the LLC in order to protect the title insurance policy.

Another important fact when holding property in an LLC is to make sure the LLC is formed and registered in the state where the property is located. Most states will not enforce the laws for eviction or other legal issues if the LLC is not registered and formed in the state of the property.

Another thing to consider is protecting your anonymity when setting up your LLCs. Real estate investors, unaware of how to set up an anonymous LLC, find themselves at greater risk of aggressive attorneys than those who know how to keep their ownership information private. When creating an LLC, there are two options: member-managed or manager-managed. This decision affects the information collected by the Secretary of State where your LLC is organized. In most cases, either the manager or the members of the LLC will have their personal information made publicly available to anyone desiring this information.

The preferred method to keep ownership or management information for your real estate LLCs completely confidential is to use an anonymity-compliant LLC as the member-manager of your state-specific real estate LLC. An anonymity-compliant LLC does not collect any information on the LLC's manager or members; thus, nothing collected translates into nothing disclosed. When using this combination, a real estate investor can own and control multiple LLCs without anyone discovering their involvement.

So again, to avoid personal liability from your investment properties, place each of them in separate LLCs. Some people think that insurance is all you need. Well, insurance only goes so far, and depends on the type of claim or coverage amount.

Chapter 5

Four Financial Benefits

In this chapter we will discuss and explore in detail the four financial benefits of real estate investments. They are as follows:

1) Cash Flow, Income

2) Principle Reduction

3) Appreciation

4) Tax savings

So let's start by looking at an example. Let's compare Investor A and Investor B.

Investor A had $50,000 to invest and decided to put it in the stock market. Investor B also had $50,000 to invest and decided to buy real estate. Here are the results after the first year.

INVESTOR A

Amount invested	$50,000
1^{St} year annual return	10%
Current value	$55,000

INVESTOR B

Purchase price	$250,000
Down Payment	50,000
Cash flow	3,168
Mortgage reduction	3,226
Appreciation	9,750
ROI	$16,144
Rate of return	32.3%

Investor B is a client of mine and those are the exact numbers for their property at the end of year one. So let's look at the four financial benefits.

Income, cash flow.

Gross rental income	$25,200
Operating expenses	(9,976)
Net operating income	$15,324
Mortgage payments	(12,156)
Net cash flow	**$3,168**

Principle reduction

Mortgage amount	$200,000
Interest rate	4.5%
Term	30 yrs
Payment	$1,013
Mortgage balance end year 1	$196,774
Principle Reduction	**$3,226**

Appreciation

Value at the time of purchase	$250,000
Value at the end of year one	$259,750
Appreciation	**$9.750**

Tax savings

Operating Income	$15,324
Interest on mortgage	(8,930)
Depreciation	(9,515)
Investment property loss	$ (3,121)
Tax Savings @ 28%	**$874**

If you notice I didn't include the tax savings in the original example but here are the four benefits for Investor B.

Cash flow	$3,168
Principle reduction	3,226
Appreciation	9,750
Tax savings	874
Total	$17.018

ROI 17,018 / 50,000 **34.0%**

In a later chapter we will discuss the tax rules and allowances for real estate but let's take a look at Depreciation or Cost Recovery as the IRS refers to it in regards to real estate. As you can see in the numbers, the biggest deduction for tax savings is depreciation. So how does that work? Depreciation or Cost Recovery is a non cash deduction where the IRS allows us to write off the price that we paid for the property over a set number of years. The following are the terms that are allowed for real estate transactions.

Commercial Property	39 years
Residential Rental Property	27.5 years
Land Improvements	15 years
Personal Property	5 years
Land	0 years

As you can see, it is important to break the purchased property down into 4 parts in order to maximize the current deduction. Here is the breakdown of the property purchased by Investor B.

Purchase Price	$250,000
Building	170,000
Land	50,000
Land Improvements	20,000
Personal Property	10,000

Depreciation Deduction

Building	$170,000 / 27.5 =	$6,182
Land Improvements	20,000 / 15 =	1,333
Personal Property	10,000 / 5 =	2,000
Total Depreciation		$9,515

One thing to note is the IRS definition of Residential Rental Property says that it must have at least a month to month lease. Any shorter term leases such as a property on Airbnb would be considered a commercial property and the building would be depreciated over 39 years.

So how do I breakdown the property into the four categories? Finding the value of the land is important because you are not allowed to depreciate land. Often times you can get the land value from the public record which is acceptable by the IRS. Land improvements would be items that are on the land but not a part of the structure such as fences, pools, patios, sheds, etc. Personal property would include the appliances, furniture included in the sale, and pool equipment.

You can determine these values after the sale, however, a good way to assign value that is recognized by the IRS is as follows. I often wrote the following addendum to the contract:

Buyer and Seller agree that the purchase price of this property shall be allocated as follows:

Building	**$170,000**
Land	**50,000**
Land Improvements	**20,000**
Personal Property	**10,000**
Total	**$250,000**

All other terms and conditions remain the same.

Sellers usually don't object because it doesn't affect the price that they receive.

Chapter 6

Mortgage or Pay Cash

One of the questions frequently asked by investors, is should I pay cash or get a mortgage? My answer is almost always the same, get a mortgage. If you remember in an earlier example I showed you that if the primary objective is cash flow then paying cash will generate a higher cash on cash return. But, even when my investor has a lot of cash to invest I will advise them to get a mortgage.

Let's say an investor tells you they have $250,000 to invest and would like to buy a property. I would immediately suggest that instead of buying one property for $250,000, they should consider putting $50,000 down and buy five properties. If the investor buys one property and goes a few months without a tenant, they have no income. If they own five properties and one goes a few months without a tenant they still have income from the other properties.

What if the investor says that they are not sure if they could qualify for five mortgages? I had that exact scenario a few years ago. This is why a good mortgage team member is important. My lender gathered all of the financial information from the client and presented this plan. He told them to buy the first property, secure a one year lease and then apply for the second mortgage. The lender can then use the rent income to offset the first mortgage and if there is a positive cash flow it might even improve the investors qualifications.

The name of the game is to create the best ROI possible for the long term investment. Let's go back to Investor B. In that example we saw that their first year ROI was **32.3%.** So what would it be if they had paid cash?

Cash investment	$250,000
Net operating income	$15,324
Appreciation	$9,750
25074 / 250000 = ROI	**10%**

I always like to point out to my investors that if they have at least a breakeven or positive cash flow, the mortgage is being paid by the tenant.

Like we always say in real estate, everyone is buying a house, it's just that some people are buying it for someone else.

Here is some information you need to know to begin the process of mortgaging your investment property.

Real estate financing includes the pledge of real property as collateral to back up a borrower's promise to repay the loan. If a default occurs, the lender is legally entitled to force the sale of the pledged property to recover the balance owed.

The financing relationship is described in terms of rights pledged as collateral for a loan. Borrowers pledge their rights to a lender but continue to own and control the property throughout the term of the loan. In this relationship, the lender holds equitable title (less than legal) to the property, which can be perfected into full legal ownership if the borrower defaults. Thus, a borrower may live in, rent out, and otherwise continue to use and benefit from the property that is itself encumbered by the lien of a real estate loan.

This explains one of the basic attractions of real estate as an investment vehicle. An owner may control a large amount of property with relatively little amount of money. This process, known as leverage, is the use of small amounts of money to control variable amounts of property through financing.

Leverage gives investors a powerful tool for the potential accumulation of large estates in their lifetimes. In fact, many investors strive to apply leverage to the greatest extent possible in order to control many highly valued properties with a minimum amount of their own money. This approach acts to preserve an investor's liquid assets, which can then be used to solve problems that inevitably arise in the course of property ownership and management.

There is a basic difference between lending for homeownership and for investment purposes. In lending for homeownership the income to repay the loan comes from the individual borrower. This is why lenders are concerned with the borrower's credit score and job history. Commercial lending

Real Estate As An Investment

differs in that the funds to repay the loan come not from the individual borrower, but from the property. It is the net operating income of the investment property that is used to repay the loan. This is why the lenders are more concerned with the property's operating statement than with the individual borrower.

Commercial property lenders require that the net operating income (NOI) from the property cover the debt service (principle and interest) a specific number of times. Common debt coverage ratios range from 1.2 to 1.5. So if the debt service is $20,000 per year, then the net operating income must be at least $24,000 per year. This insures that the property can repay the loan or provide an income to the lender in case of foreclosure. The more equity you have in the property, the less concerned the lender is about the debt ratio.

When property is pledged as collateral for a loan, three basic forms are utilized to establish the desired lender-borrower relationship, depending on which state you are in. The basic forms are the note and mortgage, deed of trust, and contract for deed.

The note and mortgage form of financing requires that the mortgagor pledge the property and all the rights therein to a mortgagee in exchange for a loan. The borrower retains legal ownership, while the lender secures an equitable interest in the collateral, an interest that can be become full legal if the borrower defaults. In this form of finance, the **note** is the actual contract for the repayment of the debt, while the **mortgage** is the pledge of real estate to secure the promise to repay. A note by itself is legal evidence of a debt and stipulates the conditions of the loan and the terms of repayment. A mortgage always needs a note to be legally enforceable, and it describes the collateral and rights being pledged.

The note and deed used to establish a **deed of trust** financing relationship parallels the note and mortgage, with one exception. With the deed of trust, the borrower-trustor actually deeds the legal fee in the collateral to a third-party trustee to hold in trust subject to the lien of the lender-beneficiary. When the loan is paid in full, the trustee reconveys the property to the trustor. With a contract for deed, this form of financing is utilized primarily between individual lenders and borrowers, not with banks.

A **contract for deed** is not accompanied by a note, but is a single complete agreement, granting physical possession to the buyer-borrower at the same time that it establishes the financing agreement with the seller-lender.

The most common type of financing for investment property today is a conventional loan. With this type of loan the lender will offset the risk by requiring the borrower to invest a prescribed amount of personal funds. The most common equity requirements are 20 to 25 % allowing a conventional mortgage to be place at about 80% of the property's value. A borrower who has invested funds of 20 to 25% would be unlikely to undermine the value of the property or walk away from it.

The information described in this chapter is the reason I recommend that you have a strong mortgage lender on your team. They will give you good advice on the type of financing that works best for the investment property.

Tom Whitehouse

PART TWO

VALUING INVESTMENT REAL ESTATE

Chapter 7

Methods of Valuation

In this section we examine the methods of determining the value of residential investment real estate. As a real estate professional working with investors, helping them understand how much they should be willing to pay for the property, considering their objectives, is the most important role you play. We will create a formula that will allow us to quickly determine the price that the investor should be willing to pay to obtain the desired ROI.

I am frequently ask, "is it a good time to invest in real estate?" My answer is always the same, yes. That's because when you have a formula to evaluate the property, you plug in the numbers, if it works you buy it if it doesn't you don't, and there will always be properties that work in any market.

Every market is unique but the basic principles of real estate investing apply everywhere and anytime. The key is to combine income, expenses and financing into a complete package that works. There is no right or wrong method of valuing real estate investments but some are certainly better and more accurate than others.

As we begin evaluating the property we will look at the four financial benefits discussed in an earlier chapter.

Income or cash flow – The amount of cash the property produces after paying the operating expenses and mortgage payment. This is a key number for valuation.

Principal reduction – This is the mortgage loan being paid down by the tenant. This benefit is not realized until sometime in the future when the property is sold or refinanced.

Income tax savings – The key factor is depreciation. This benefit can vary depending on the investor's tax bracket and the tax laws can change. It's important to stay up to date on the applicable tax laws, and the accountant team member can assist.

Appreciation – This is the increase in market value that also will not be realized until sometime in the future.

So let's look at the most common valuation methods used and their strengths and weaknesses.

Price per Unit – This method doesn't take into account any variables such as income or expenses. This method would only be of value if every unit in the building was identical and even then, it is not very reliable.

Price per Square Foot – This method doesn't account for the income or expenses. It could be very misleading considering two properties with the same square footage could have very different operating cost.

Gross Rent Multiplier – This method seems to be used often by investors and is sometimes referred to as the 1% rule. Some will say, "I'll pay 10 times the gross annual rent." Or if the monthly rent is $2400, I'll pay $240,000 (1%). Again, can you imagine two properties that have the same annual or monthly rent but very different operating cost?

Cash on Cash – This method is widely used and it does take into account the income and expenses but it is difficult to translate this into a price.

Capitalization Rate – This method, also referred to as **Cap Rate,** is by far the most accurate way to determine the value of real estate investment property. It takes into consideration the income and expenses and creates a formula that can be used to quickly determine the appropriate price for the subject property.

Chapter 8

Capitalization Rate Explained

So what is the Cap Rate? It is calculated by dividing the net operating income by the price paid.

If we look back again at **Investor B**:

Annual Income $25,200

Operating Expenses   - $9,867

Operating Profit $15,324

Price paid $250,000

$15,324 / $250,000 = **6.2%** Cap rate

So how do we know if that is a good rate? Capitalization rates will vary in different locations and different markets. You'll need to determine the rate in your market area.

So I went into the MLS and selected 12 different communities to determine the Cap Rate in each. First I pulled recent sales in those communities of similar properties. Next I pulled recent rentals of the same type of properties to get the average rent. Below are a couple of examples of the data.

River Marina community:

Current average rent $1700/mo.	$20,400
Operating cost (40%)	- $8,160
Net operating profit	$12,240
Recent average sales	$180,000
Cap rate	$12,240 / $180,000 = **6.8%**

Martin Crossing Townhouses:

Current average rent $1600/mo.	$19,200
Operating cost (40%)	- $7,680
Net operating profit	$11,520
Recent average sales	$175,000

Cap rate $11,520 / $175,000 = **6.6%**

After calculating this data for the 12 communities I found that the cap rate ranged from 6.2% to 6.8%. I decided that the appropriate rate for my area would be 6.5%.

Often times an investor will have a cap rate in mind and you'll have to go through the data to help them understand the rate in the area.

I had an investor named John that met me in my office one day and he explained that he had recently sold a company and now wanted to invest the money in real estate. He told me that he really knows what he is doing, he had attended many seminars, and read many books on real estate investing. He then explained that he would only accept property with a cap rate of 10%. I asked him where he got that number and he said from the books and seminars. I then politely told him that cap rates are different in every area and the current rate here is 6.5%. He looked disappointed but when I shared some recent properties that my investors had purchased with a 6.5% average cap rate and then showed him the ROI of 30% +, he thought for a minute and then said "let's do it."

The question then is, can an investor get a higher cap rate than the average? Of course, but just like the stock market, to get a higher than average return you must be willing to accept what? Higher risk.

So what do I mean by "higher risk"? For most investors that I work with, I recommend that they buy properties that are in neighborhoods or buildings where most of the properties are owner occupied. Those are the types of properties that I used in calculating the Cap rate of 6.5%. If you invest in properties that are in a neighborhood or building that is primarily occupied by tenants, the Cap rate might be as high as 10%. This is the result of the price of the property being lower in relation to the rental income. But here is the risk. In those properties you will very likely have more turnover of tenants and as a result more days or even weeks of vacancies, which lowers the rental income. It is very Important to look at the Return on Investment to make sure the return is acceptable.

In addition, the larger issue with the ROI is the appreciation. With properties that are in an area that are mostly owner occupied, your investment property appreciates just like the others. The value goes up with the market. In a community where most are owned by investors, the only way that your property will increase in value is if the Net Income increases. As a result your rental income will have to increase at a much higher rate than your expenses. This will usually result in lower appreciation.

On the following page I have an included an example of an investment worksheet that you can create to capture all of the information about the property in order to calculate the four benefits and the return on investment.

Tom Whitehouse

INVESTMENT WORKSHEET

PROPERTY INFORMATION

Purchase Cost _____

Cash invested _____

Financing: Amount _____ P&I _____ per mo.

Land Cost _____ Depreciation

Personal Prop _____ Yrs. _____ _____

Building Cost _____ Yrs. _____ _____

Land Improvement _____ Yrs. _____ _____

Total Depreciation _____

INCOME AND EXPENSES

Annual Gross Operating Income _____

RE Tax _____ Mngt _____ Insurance _____

Repairs _____ Advertising _____ Misc. _____

Total Operating Expense _____

THE FOUR BENEFITS

I. Gross Operating Income _____
minus : Operating Expenses − _____
equals: Net Operating Inc = _____
minus: Annual Debt Service − _____
equals: **Cash Flow Before Tax** = _____

II. Annual Debt Service _____
minus: Interest − _____
equals: **Principal Reduction** = _____

III. Net Operating Income _____
minus: Interest   - _____
minus: Total Depreciation - _____
equals: Taxable Income   = _____
multiplied by: Tax Bracket x _____ %
equals: **Tax Saved**   =   _____

IV. **Appreciation** (estimate)   _____

RATES OF RETURN

Return on Investment with Appreciation

Cash Flow before Tax + Prin. Reduction+ Tax Saved+ Appr.

Cash Invested	=	_____ %

Return on Investment without Appreciation

Cash Flow before Tax + Prin. Reduction + Tax Saved

Cash Invested	=	_____ %

Capitalization Rate

Net Operating Income
Purchased Cost   = _____ %

Cash on Cash

Cash Flow Before Tax
Cash Invested   = _____ %

Tom Whitehouse

Chapter 9

How Much Should I Pay For The Property

We are now ready to develop a formula to help our investors determine how much they should be willing to pay for the property. The first step is to understand the economic and physical details of a property that would best meet the investment goals. The clearer the picture, the better the odds that we will recognize it when we see it. Knowing exactly what we're looking for helps sift through large numbers of properties and has the added benefit of helping us make offers quickly and confidently when you find a match.

First we need to determine the geographic location. Are we interested in a certain neighborhood, subdivision or area of town? Once we have picked the location, we'll have a clear understanding of all the factors that determine local property values and rental rates.

The next essential criteria is the property type. Are we looking for single-family homes or multifamily properties? You can acquire houses, condos and apartments individually or buy them in bunches by purchasing duplexes, fourplexes and even larger condo and apartment complexes. The conventional wisdom is that single-family homes or condo communities where most are owner occupied, offer the most reliable demand and appreciation while multifamily properties where most are tenant occupied offer the best opportunity for cash flow. By and large the value of single-family homes is set by non-investors. These individuals are buying a *home,* and emotional factors play into their willingness to buy at a certain price. Multifamily properties, in contrast, are bought and sold largely by investors, and this means that their prices are determined by the value of the rent income they produce. If the rental income doesn't increase at a higher rate than the expenses over time, then the value will not increase.

Now we go back to the investors objectives. You can buy single-family homes for appreciation and relative stability - building your net worth - or you can emphasize multifamily properties that offer multiple streams of income – building your cash flow.

So What should I pay for the property?

Once we have determined the location and type of property, we can calculate the cap rate as we discussed in a previous chapter. Using the worksheet, we can record all of the necessary information. See the example below:

Monthly rent $1800
Desired Cap rate of 6.5%
Annual income 1800 x 12 = $21,600
Operating Expenses   - $ 8,640
Net Operating Income $12,960
Formula for Price:

Net operating Income / Cap rate = Price

$12,960 / .065 = $199,385

If we purchase the property at that price, what is the cash flow and ROI?

Cash Flow:

**20% down 5% mortgage rate
Payment $856 x 12 = $10,272
Down payment $39,877**

Income	**$21,600**
Operating Expenses 40%	**- $8,640**
Income	**$12,960**
Debt Service	**- $ 10,272**
Cash Flow	**$2,688**

Net Cash Flow / Down Payment

Cash on Cash	**6.7%**

ROI:

Cash Flow	**$2,688**
Mortgage Reduction	**$2,353**
Appreciation 3.5%	**$6,978**

$12,019 / $39,877 =

Rate Of Return	**30.1%**

Real Estate As An Investment

What if I paid cash?

Purchase Price   **$199,385**

Net Operating Income   **$12,960**

Appreciation 3.5%   **$6,967**

$19,927 / $199,385 =

Rate of Return   **10.0%**

So here is how the Cap rate effects the value or price to be paid.

Net Oper. Income	Cap Rate	Value/Price
$18,000	5%	$360,000
$18,000	6%	$300,000
$18,000	7%	$257,143
$18,000	8%	$225,000

So to review. The two formulas we need to know are:

To Calculate the Cap Rate

Net Oper. Profit / Price of Property = Cap Rate

To Calculate the Price to Pay

Net Operating Profit / Cap Rate = Price

PART THREE

TIME TO MOVE THE EQUITY

Chapter 10

Evaluating Your Return On Equity

As an investor or when working with your investor clients, it is a good practice to evaluate your return on equity at least once each year. As your equity grows, the return on equity as a percentage will get smaller and at some point you'll need to look at moving the equity.

To illustrate how this works, let's refer again to Investor B from our past examples. We calculated the first year return on investment to be **32.3%.** Let's now look at the end of year two. As I mentioned earlier, these are not estimates, these are actual numbers from my clients investment.

Investor B Year Two

Cash Flow	$3,068
Mortgage Reduction	$3,375
Appreciation	$13,000
Total ROI	**$19,443**
Equity	**$66,144**

Total ROI / Equity

2nd Year ROI   **29.4%**

Even with a strong year of appreciation (5.0%), the total return as a percentage went down.

Real Estate As An Investment

Now we will look strictly at the return on equity. The appreciation will be rolled into the property value to adjust the total equity. Let's compare the year of purchase with the end of year three.

RETURN ON EQUITY

YEAR OF PURCHASE

I. Net Equity

Price Paid	**$250,000**
- Mortgage	**200,000**
= Net Equity	**$50,000**

II. Annual Benefits

Cash Flow Before Tax	**$3,168**
Principal Reduction	**3,226**
Tax Saved	**874**
Total Annual Benefit	**$7,268**

III. Current Annual Rate of Return

Total Annual Benefits	**$7,268**
Net Equity	**$50,000**
Return on Equity	**14.5%**

YEAR THREE

I. Net Equity

Current Market Value	**$272,750**
- Loan Balance	**189,800**
= Net Equity	**$82,950**

II. Current Annual Benefits

Cash Flow Before Tax	**$3,650**
Principal Reduction	**3,350**
Tax Saved	**960**
Total Annual Benefits	**$8,140**

III. Current Annual Rate of Return

Total Annual Benefits	**$8,140**
Net Equity	**$82,950**
Return on Equity	**9.8%**

As you can see the percentage of Return on Equity is going down each year. This is not a bad thing, it is simply the result of the accumulated equity that is growing each year. The combined benefits are lower as a percentage of the new equity.

This is something that we need to check at least once each year for our own portfolio and for our investor clients. I send a report each year to my clients showing them the total dollar equity position of each property as well as the rate of return. This will prompt them to make decisions about how to best use the equity which we will discuss in the next chapter.

Chapter 11

Time To Move The Equity

When the equity position of a property gets to a certain level, the owner should consider ways to use the equity to improve their return. There are basically three common ways to move the equity.

1) Sell the property

2) Refinance the property

3) Exchange the property.

Let's look at each alternative.

Sell the property – To sell the property out right or (liquidate) is usually done when an investor decides to exit their property holdings, perhaps for retirement, or a need to generate cash. The biggest problem with this is that there will be capital gains tax to be paid on the realized profit. Calculating the amount of realized gain on the property will sometimes surprise the owner.

In the following example, let's assume that the owner paid $350,000 for the property and 7 years later sold it for $450,000. That looks like a profit of $100,000. Unfortunately that's not how it works. To find the realized gain you must first adjust the Basis.

HOW TO CALCULATE REALIZED GAIN

ADJUSTED BASIS

Original Cost	**$350,000**
Plus Improvements	**4,500**
Minus Depreciation Taken	**89,245**
Equals Adjusted Basis	**$265,255**

RELALIZED GAIN

Sale Price	**$450,000**
Minus Cost of Sale	**32,000**
Minus Adjusted Basis	**265,255**
Equals Realized Gain	**$152,745**

As you can see, the gain would then be subject to capital gains tax. The "improvements" on the adjusted basis represent undepreciated cost to prepare the home for sale. The "cost of sale" in the realized gain calculation represents the closing cost.

Refinance the property – A very popular option to move and use the equity is to refinance. I've used my client referred to as Investor B several times and here's what they did to move the equity.

After they owned the property four years the home was worth $287,290 and their mortgage had been paid down (by the tenant), to $186,150 leaving them with over $100,000 of equity. If you remember they originally invested $50,000 of their own cash to buy the property. They went to their mortgage lender and refinanced with a loan and cash out of $50,000. They then purchased another property for $250,000. They now own investment real estate worth $537,000 and how much of their cash have they invested? .....$50,000.

Exchange the property - The third option to move the equity is to exchange the property through a 1031 Exchange. As you saw in the example, when we calculated the realized gain at $152,745, that would create a capital gains tax of approximately $30,000. The exchange process allows you to defer the tax.

I will describe in great detail, the Like-Kind Exchange process in the next section.

PART FOUR

1031 EXCHANGE

Tom Whitehouse

Chapter 12

Tax Benefits of Exchange

The 1031 Exchange, often referred to as a Like-Kind Exchange, has been around for many years but is one of the most under- utilized tax benefits in the Tax Code. Many investors don't understand it and the tremendous tax saving benefits that are available.

When you sell an investment property, you'll likely pay substantial capital gains taxes at the time of the sale if you have a gain. As shown in the previous chapter, after calculating the basis of the property you are selling, you might end up with a substantial taxable gain. The amount of tax will vary based on your income, but it will likely be 15%-20% federal tax on the gain. Depending on where you live, the gain could also be taxed as income at the state level. In addition, accumulated depreciation recapture is taxed at a federal rate of 25% and varies at the state level. In some cases capital gains tax can reach 30% or more.

However, you will not owe any taxes at the time of sale if you execute a 1031 Deferred Exchange correctly. I have often heard it referred to as a "tax free" exchange. While it is not tax free, the tax can be deferred indefinitely if you invest the proceeds in a new property or properties of equal or greater value and maintain the same or higher loan amount.

There are no limits as to how many times or how frequently you can do a 1031 Deferred Exchange as long as you hold the property long enough with the IRS, for at least two tax periods. Theoretically, you could do it forever, selling properties and then reinvesting in like-kind properties, deferring taxes and building equity and value over time.

At the time of inheritance, your heirs will also benefit from an IRS rule that allows them a "stepped -up" basis; this means the basis at the time of inheritance is the current market value, essentially eliminating the gain and related taxes forever.

Like-kind doesn't mean a house for a house, it just means the new investment has to be real estate. You can sell a house and reinvest in vacant land, or sell a house and buy three houses. I like to think of it being like the game of Monopoly. Buy a house, buy another house, buy another house, sell the houses and buy a hotel.

Recent changes in tax laws eliminated all exchange types except for real estate. This is a win for investors because you can exchange a single-family home in a high cost market and purchase a portfolio of rental properties in a lower more affordable state. This will create improved cash flow, which generates greater returns.

You also have the ability to reset your depreciation. As we discussed in previous chapters, you can depreciate rental property over 27.5 years. Your depreciation is based on the cost you paid for the property and doesn't increase as the property value increases. When you sell and exchange the property you start over with 27.5 years and with the higher value property giving you greater tax deductions.

As I said earlier, there is no cap on how many times you can do a 1031 Exchange. That means you can turn a duplex into a fourplex into a single-family rental property into a real estate empire.

Chapter 13

The Exchange Process

   The tax deferred exchange, as defined by paragraph 1031 of the Internal Revenue Code, offers taxpayers one of the last great opportunities to build wealth and save taxes. By completing the exchange, the Taxpayer (Exchanger) can dispose of investment property, acquire Replacement Property and defer the tax that would ordinarily be due upon the sale. To fully defer the capital gain or recapture tax, the Exchanger must (a) acquire "like kind" Replacement Property that will be held for investment or used productively in a trade or business, (b) purchase Replacement Property of equal or greater value , (c) reinvest all of the equity into the Replacement Property, and (d) obtain the same or greater debt on the replacement property. Debt may be replaced with additional cash, but cash equity cannot be replaced with additional debt. Additionally, the Exchanger may not receive cash or other benefits from the sale proceeds during the sale. In simple terms, the debt on the new property must be equal to or greater than the debt on the sold property and no cash can be received from the sale.

An exchange is rarely a swap of properties between two parties. Most exchanges involve multiple parties: the Exchanger, the buyer of the Exchanger's old (relinquished) property, the seller of the Exchanger's new (replacement) property, and a Qualified Intermediary. To create the exchange and obtain the benefit of the "Safe Harbor" protections set out in Treasury Regulations 1.1031(k)-1(g)(4) which prevent actual or constructive receipt of exchange funds, prudent taxpayers use a professional Qualified Intermediary. We'll explain their role later in the chapter.

Tax Deferred Exchange Terminology

As with any other specific area of law, tax deferred exchanges have their own language, which may be confusing to those who are unfamiliar with these transactions. The following are some of the exchange terms and phrases that are often used with their "plain-English" interpretations.

Basis (Adjusted Basis): The amount paid for a property taking into consideration added value for capital improvements and decreased by the amount of depreciation taken (or allowable); it is the value of a property for tax purposes.

Boot: The fair market value of any non-qualified property received in exchange. While receipt of boot will not necessarily disqualify the exchange, an Exchanger who receives Boot in an exchange transaction generally recognizes gain to the value of the Boot received. Some common examples of Boot are: cash, debt relief that is not offset with new debt, property intended for personal use, and property which is neither like-kind nor like-class to the Relinquished Property.

Constructive Receipt: A term referring to the control or ability to receive proceeds by an Exchanger even though funds may not be directly in the Exchanger's possession.

Exchange Accommodation Titleholder: The person or entity used to facilitate a "reverse" or "improvement" exchange. The Exchange Accommodation Titleholder (EAT) will hold (park) title to either the Relinquished or the Replacement Property during the exchange.

Exchange Period: The period during which the Exchanger must acquire Replacement Property in the exchange. The exchange period starts on the date the Exchanger transfers the first Relinquished Property and ends on the earlier of the 180th day thereafter or the due date (including extensions) for filing the Exchanger's tax return for the year of the Relinquished Property transfer.

Exchanger or Taxpayer: The property owner seeking to defer capital gain, recapture, or other income tax by utilizing a IRC paragraph 1031 exchange.

Forward Exchange: The most common form of exchange transaction in which the exchange begins with the sale of the Relinquished Property to a buyer and concludes with the purchase of Replacement Property from a seller (typically a third party).

Identification Period: The period during which the Exchanger must identify Replacement Property in the exchange. The Identification Period starts on the day the Exchanger transfers the first Relinquished Property and ends at midnight on the 45th day thereafter.

Improvement Exchange: An exchange in which improvements are made to the Replacement Property prior to acquisition by the Exchanger, either using exchange funds or funds lent by the Exchanger (or lender) to the Exchanged Accommodation Titleholder.

Like-Kind Property: Generally, all real property located within the United States is considered to be "like-kind" to all other U.S. real property as long as the Exchanger's intent is to hold the properties as an investment or for the productive use in a trade or business.

Qualified Intermediary: The person or entity that facilitates the exchange for the Exchanger. Although the Treasury Regulations use the term "Qualified Intermediary," other common terms are "exchange facilitator", or "exchange accommodator". To be a Qualified Intermediary, the exchange facilitator must meet certain criteria spelled out in Tres. Reg. 1.1031(k)-1(g)(4).

Realized Gain: The amount realized from the sale of property which is potentially subject to tax, it equals the gross sale price minus the closing cost minus the adjusted basis.

Recognized Gain: The amount of the realized gain that is subject to tax. In a taxable sale, (no 1031 exchange), the realized gain is all recognized. In a fully deferred 1031 exchange, no gain is recognized; the realized gain is deferred.

Relinquished Property: The "old" property divested (sold) by the exchanger.

Replacement Property: The "new" property acquired (purchased) by the exchanger.

Reverse Exchange: An exchange involving an Exchange Accommodation Titleholder (EAT) when it is necessary for the Replacement Property to be acquired before the Relinquished Property can be sold to a Buyer, or when improvements must be made to the Replacement Property before it can be acquired by the Exchanger.

Tom Whitehouse

The Exchange Process

Timing is important. Certain actions must be taken in sequence and exchanges must be completed within strict time limits.

1. Prior to closing the sale of the Relinquished Property, the Exchanger and the Qualified Intermediary must enter into an Exchange Agreement which requires the Qualified Intermediary to (a) acquire the Relinquished Property from the Exchanger and transfer it to the buyer (by direct deed from Exchanger to Buyer), and (b) to acquire the Replacement Property from the Seller and transfer it to the Exchanger (by direct deed from the seller to Exchanger).

2. Also prior to closing the sale of the Relinquished Property, the Exchanger must assign rights under the Relinquished Property sale contract to the Qualified Intermediary and provide notice of assignment to the buyer.

3. At closing, net proceeds from the Relinquished Property sale (exchange funds) are paid directly to the Qualified Intermediary, to be held in a separate account for the benefit of the Exchanger until used to purchase Replacement Property.

4. The Exchanger has 45 days from the date the Relinquished Property is transferred to identify potential Replacement Properties. Identification must be specific and unambiguous, in writing, signed by the Exchanger, and delivered to the Qualified Intermediary or another party to the transaction as permitted by Treas. Reg. 1.1031(k)-1©(2) prior to the end of the 45 day Identification period.. The list of identified potential Replacement Properties cannot be changed after the 45th day; the Exchanger may only acquire from the list of identified properties. If no property is identified, the exchange funds will be returned to the Exchanger after the 45th day.

5. Prior to closing the sale of the Replacement Property, the Exchanger must assign rights under the Replacement Property purchase contract to the Qualified Intermediary and provide notice of assignment to the seller.

6. The Exchanger authorizes the Qualified Intermediary to wire the funds directly to the seller or closing agent for purchase of Replacement Property, and the seller transfers title directly to the Exchanger, completing the exchange.

7. Purchase of Replacement Property must be completed by the earlier of the 180th day after transfer of the first Relinquished Property or the due date (including extensions) for filing Exchanger's tax return. Any unspent exchange funds will be returned to the Exchanger at termination of the exchange.

The key to a successful exchange is to plan ahead.

Step 1. Contact a Qualified Intermediary. In advance of the closing date, after entering into the purchase and the sale agreement, advise them of your intent to do an exchange. They will then prepare the appropriate Exchange Agreement, Assignments, and other documents that must be executed prior to closing on the Relinquished Property being sold.

Step 2. Include an "Exchange Cooperation Clause" in the purchase and sale agreement. See examples below.

Step 3. Start searching for acceptable Replacement Property immediately to ensure that you can meet the strict time frame for the 45 day Identification Period.

Exchange Cooperation Clauses for Contracts

Relinquished Property Sale Contract

"Notwithstanding anything to the contrary, Buyer hereby acknowledges that it is the intent of Seller to effect an IRC 1031 tax deferred exchange, which will not delay the closing or cause additional expense to Buyer. Seller's rights under this agreement may be assigned to the Qualified Intermediary for the purpose of completing such an exchange. Buyer agrees to cooperate with Seller and the Intermediary in a manner necessary to complete the exchange."

Replacement Property Purchase Contract

"Notwithstanding anything to the contrary, Seller hereby acknowledges that it is the intent of Buyer to effect an IRC 1031 tax deferred exchange, which will not delay the closing or cause additional expense to Seller. Buyer's rights under this agreement may be assigned to the Qualified Intermediary for the purpose of completing such an exchange. Seller agrees to cooperate with Buyer and Intermediary in a manner necessary to complete the exchange.

The most common exchange structure is the delayed "forward" exchange in which the Relinquished Property is sold, the proceeds (Exchange Funds) are delivered to the Qualified Intermediary, and are subsequently used to acquire Replacement Property from a third party seller. Two critical requirements in a delayed exchange are that the Replacement Property must be properly identified within the Identification Period and acquired before the end of the Exchange Period.

There are two key deadlines that the Exchanger must meet to have a valid exchange:

Identification Period: Within 45 calendar days of the transfer of the first Relinquished Property, the Exchanger must identify the Replacement Property to be acquired.

Exchange Period: The Exchanger must receive the Replacement Property within the earlier of 180 calendar days after the date on which the Exchanger transferred the first Relinquished Property, or the due date (including extensions) for the Exchanger's tax return for the tax year in which the transfer occurs.

The time period for the 45-day Identification Period and the 180-day Exchange Period are very strict and cannot be extended even if the 45th day or 180th day falls on a Saturday, Sunday or legal holiday.

The requirements for a Proper Identification Notice must include a specific and unambiguous description of the Replacement Property, must be signed by the Exchanger and must include the legal description, a street address or distinguishable building name.

Exchangers have the flexibility to identify multiple and alternative Replacement Properties.

Three Property Rule: The Exchanger may identify as potential Replacement Property any three properties, without regard to their fair market value.

200% Rule: The exchanger may identify as potential Replacement Property any number of properties, provided the aggregate fair market value of all of the identified properties does not exceed 200% of the aggregate fair market value of all the Relinquished Properties.

The "reverse" exchange occurs when the taxpayer acquires the replacement property before transferring the relinquished property. A "pure" reverse exchange, where the taxpayer owns both the relinquished and replacement properties at the same time, is not permitted. The IRS has provided guidance on structuring a reverse exchange, offering a safe harbor under Rev. Proc. 2000-37. An Exchange Accommodation Title Holder (EAT), acquires and holds the target property (the parked property) in a special purpose entity, typically a single member LLC. To complete a reverse exchange, the EAT will take title to either the Relinquished Property or the Replacement Property under a "Qualified Exchange Accommodation Arrangement."

The same 45 day Identification Period and 180 day Exchange Period deadlines apply to a safe harbor reverse exchange with a slight tweak. If the EAT has begun the exchange by acquiring the Replacement Property, then the Exchanger must identify within 45 days after the EAT's acquisition of the parked property, one or more Relinquished Properties to be exchanged for the Replacement Property. The identification rules require that written identification be delivered to another party to the exchange, such as the EAT or the Qualified Intermediary, identification permitted under the three property or 200% rules. The identified Relinquished Property must be sold, and the parked Replacement Property transferred to the Exchanger to complete the exchange within 180 days of parking the Replacement Property with the EAT.

Tom Whitehouse

Chapter 14

Other Exchange Considerations

Do Vacation and Second Homes qualify for IRC 1031 treatment? It has been established that vacation or second homes held by the Exchanger primarily for personal use do not qualify for tax deferred exchange treatment.

The safe harbor for a vacation or second home to qualify as **Relinquished** Property in a 1031 exchange requires the Exchanger to have owned it for twenty-four months immediately before the exchange, and within each of those two 12-month periods the Exchanger must have 1) rented the unit at fair market rental for fourteen or more days, and 2) restricted personal use to the greater of fourteen days or ten percent of the number of days it was rented at fair market rental within that 12-month period.

The safe harbor for a vacation or second home to qualify as **Replacement** Property in a 1031 exchange requires the Exchanger to own the vacation home for twenty four months immediately after the exchange, and for each of those 12 month periods the Exchanger must 1) rent the unit at fair market rental for fourteen or more days, and 2) restrict personal use to the greater of fourteen days or ten percent of the number of days it was rented at fair market rental within that 12 month period.

"Personal use" includes use by the Exchanger's friends and family members that do not pay fair market value rent, but would not include use as a related party's primary residence if the related party pays rent at a fair market rate.

What about ownership as an LLC?

Because of the advantageous tax treatment combined with liability protection, limited liability companies have become a preferred way to own real estate in the United States. By understanding this structure, they can also be used to provide flexibility in complying with the requirements of a

1031 exchange. All 50 states have enacted laws permitting the formation of LLCs, including single member LLCs. Although they are separate entities (from their owners) for legal and liability purposes, they may be disregarded entities for federal tax purposes. That means that although the member of a single member LLC is insulated from liability from the LLCs activities, the sole member is considered to be the tax payer for federal tax purposes. This creates planning opportunities for 1031 exchanges.

For federal tax purposes, an LLC is characterized as a sole proprietorship (which reports income on a schedule C, D, E or F to Form 1040), a partnership (which reports income on Form 1065) or a corporation (which reports income on Form 1120 or Form 1120-S). If the LLC makes no election with the IRS to be treated differently, by default, a single member LLC is considered to be a sole proprietorship and therefore is disregarded from its member for federal tax purposes.

Similarly, an LLC with two of more members that makes no election with the IRS is considered to be a partnership for federal tax purposes. An exception to this rule provides that the IRS will consider an LLC owned solely by a husband and wife as community property to be a disregarded entity. This only applies in the community property states. An LLC owned solely by husband and wife would be considered to be a partnership in the non-community property states.

In addition to the default rules referenced above, an LLC (either single member or multi-member) can make an election with the IRS to be treated as a corporation for tax purposes. If desired, the LLC can make a further election to be treated as an S corporation instead of a C corporation. In summary, an LLC with only one owner will be classified as a disregarded entity or a corporation; whereas an LLC with two or more members will be classified as a partnership or a corporation (unless it is a husband and wife LLC in a community property state).

The use of disregarded entities can be helpful in resolving challenges which may be presented by the vesting requirements for a valid 1031 exchange; i.e, the Replacement Property must be acquired by the same taxpayer that disposed of the Relinquished Property.

Treasury regulations provide that single member LLCs that acquire property are ignored for federal tax purposes and that the member is treated as the direct owner of the property. The IRS rules state that the disposition of the Relinquished Property (or acquisition of the Replacement Property) by a disregarded entity of the tax payer will be treated for purposes of 1031 as a direct disposition or acquisition of the property by the taxpayer. The key to understanding the use of disregarded entities in a 1031 exchange context is the identification of the taxpayer. To have a valid 1031 exchange, the same taxpayer must sell the Relinquished Property and acquire the Replacement Property. For example, assume a taxpayer wants to exchange a Relinquished Property that he owns individually; but he wants to acquire the Replacement Property in a single member LLC to protect himself from liability. Because of the disregarded treatment of single member LLCs for tax purpose, this is not a problem.

Related Party Exchanges.

Related Parties: Related parties are defined as persons or entities bearing a relationship to the Exchanger, such as members of a family; a grantor and fiduciary of any trust; two corporations which are members of the same controlled group; and corporations and partnerships with more than 50% direct or indirect common ownership in the entities.

Two-Year Holding Period; Under the 1031 code it is clear that two related parties, owning separate properties, may swap those properties with one another and defer the recognition of gain as long as both parties hold their Replacement Properties for two years following the exchange. This rule was imposed to prevent taxpayers from using exchanges to shift the tax basis between the properties to avoid paying taxes upon the subsequent sale of one of the properties.

Related Seller: Exchanges in which the Replacement Property seller is the related party are not likely to qualify for tax deferral unless the related party seller also does an exchange. Under IRS rules, exchange treatment will be denied to and Exchanger who, through a Qualified Intermediary, acquires Replacement Property from a related party seller that receives cash or other non-like-kind property, regardless of whether the Exchanger holds the Replacement Property for the requisite two years. The IRS will generally view this transaction as yielding the same result as if the Exchanger swapped properties with a related party, and then the related party immediately sold the property acquired, violating the two year holding requirement. The related party rules cannot be avoided by interposing an unrelated Qualified Intermediary.

Related Buyer: The IRS has clarified that there is no basis shifting or tax avoidance when the taxpayer, through an unrelated Qualified Intermediary, transfers Relinquished Property to a related buyer, but acquires Replacement Property from an unrelated seller. The exchange likely will be respected even if the related buyer voluntarily disposes of the property it acquired from the taxpayer within two years of acquisition. The IRS rational was that only the taxpayer owned property before the exchange and the taxpayer continued to be invested in like-kind property following the exchange. Because the related parties did not own property prior to the exchange, its subsequent disposal would not result in cashing out or basis-shifting by the taxpayer.

Tom Whitehouse

Estimating the 1031 Tax Deferral on the Sale of Investment Property

This formula is a guide to estimate the potential capital gain tax owed on the transfer of property.

1. **First, calculate the adjusted basis:**

	Original Price		$ _____
Plus	Improvements	+	$ _____
Equals		=	$ _____
Minus	Depreciation	-	$ _____
Equals	Adjusted Basis	=	$ _____

2. Second, use the Adjusted Basis to determine the Capital Gain Tax:

	Sale Price	$ _____
Minus	Adjusted Basis	- $ _____
Equals	Adj Sale Price	= $ _____
Minus	Transaction Cost	- $ _____
Equals	**Total Gain on Sale**	= $ _____
Times	St. Cap Gain Tax %	x $ _____
Equals **(A)**	**St Cap Gain Tax**	= $ _____
	Gain from Sale	= $ _____
Times	Fed Capital Gains %	x $ _____
Equals **(B) Tax on gain from sale**		= $ _____
	Gain from Depreciation	= $ _____
Times	Fed tax on Depreciation	x 25%
Equals **(C) Tax on Depreciation**		= $ _____
Total Tax A + B + C		= $ _____

though Tom Whitehouse

PART FIVE

TAX STRATEGY FOR INVESTMENT REAL ESTATE

Tom Whitehouse

Chapter 15

Reporting Income

In most cases, you must include in your gross income all amounts you receive as rent. Rental income is any payment you receive for the use or occupation of property. It isn't limited to amounts you receive as normal rental payments.

The following are common types of rental income.

Advance rent. Advance rent is any amount you receive before the period that it covers. Include advance rent in your rental income in the year you receive, regardless of the period covered or the method of accounting you use.

Example. On June 1, 2020 you received the 1st month's rent and the last month's rent for a one year contract. The last month's rent must be included in your rental income for 2020.

Expenses paid by tenant. If your tenant pays any of your expenses, those payments are rental income. Because you must include this amount in income, you can also deduct the expenses if they are deductible rental expenses.

Example. Your tenant pay the water and sewage bill for your rental property and deducts the amount from the normal rent payment. Under the terms of the lease, your tenant doesn't have to pay this bill. Include the utility bill paid by the tenant and any amount received as a rent payment in your rental income. You can deduct the utility payment made by your tenant as a rental expense.

Security deposits. Don't include a security deposit in your income when you receive it if you plan to return it to your tenant at the end of the lease. But if you keep part or all of the security deposit during any year because your tenant doesn't live up to the terms of the lease, include the amount you keep in your income when you receive it.

Lease with option to buy. If the rental agreement gives your tenant the right to buy your rental property, the payments you receive under the agreement generally are rental income. If your tenant exercises the right to buy the property, the payments you receive for the period after the date of sale are considered part of the selling price.

Tom Whitehouse

Chapter 16

Deductible Expenses

You generally deduct your rental expenses in the year you pay them.

Listed below are the most common rental expenses.

- Advertising
- Auto and travel expense
- Cleaning and maintenance
- Commissions
- Depreciation

- Insurance
- Interest
- Legal and professional fees
- Local transportation expenses
- Management fees
- Mortgage interest paid to banks
- Rental payments
- Repairs
- Taxes
- Utilities

Some of these expenses as well as other less common ones are described below.

Depreciation. Depreciation is a capital expense. It is the mechanism for recovering your cost in an income-producing property and must be taken over the expected life of the property. You can begin to depreciate rental property when it is ready and available for rent. I will address this later in more detail.

Interest expense. You can deduct mortgage interest you pay on your rental property. If you refinance the property for more than the previous balance, you can deduct the entire amount as long as the proceeds are used for the rental property.

Local transportation expenses. You may be able to deduct your ordinary and necessary local transportation expenses if you incur them to collect rental income or to manage, conserve or maintain your rental property. However, transportation expenses incurred to travel between your home and a rental property generally constitute nondeductible commuting costs unless you use your home as your principle place of business for your rental property. In this case other cost related to your home office may also be deductible.

Generally, if you use your personal car, pickup truck, or light van for rental activities, you can deduct the expenses using one of two methods: actual expenses or the standard mileage rate. To deduct car expenses under either method, you must keep records of the miles driven.

Rental of property. You can deduct the rent you pay for property you use for rental purposes.

Travel expenses. You can deduct the ordinary and necessary expenses of traveling away from home if the primary purpose of the trip is to collect rental income or to manage or maintain your rental property. You must properly allocate your expenses between rental and nonrental activities.

Repairs and Improvements.

Repairs. Generally, an expense for repairing or maintaining your rental property may be deducted if you aren't required to capitalize the expense.

Improvements. You must capitalize any expense you pay to improve your rental property. An expense is for an improvement if it results in a betterment to your property, restores your property, or adapts your property to a new or different use.

Betterments. Expenses that may result in a betterment to your property include expenses for fixing a pre-existing defect or condition, enlarging or expanding your property , or increasing the capacity, strength, or quality of your property.

Restoration. Expenses that may be for restoration include expenses for replacing a substantial structural part of your property, repairing damage to your property after you properly adjusted the basis of your property as a result of a casualty loss, or rebuilding your property to a like-new condition.

Adaptation. Expenses that may be for adaptation include expenses for altering your property to a use that isn't consistent with the intended ordinary use of your property when you began renting the property.

Tom Whitehouse

Chapter 17

Depreciation of Rental Property

You recover the cost of income-producing property through yearly tax deductions. You do this by depreciating the property; that is, by deducting some of the cost each year on your tax return.

Three factors determine how much depreciation you can deduct each year: (1) your basis in the property, (2) the recovery period for the property, and (3) the depreciation method used.

You can deduct depreciation only on the part of your property used for rental purposes.

Depreciation reduces your basis for figuring gain or loss on a future sale or exchange.

You can depreciate your property if it meets all of the following requirements.

- You own the property
- You use the property in your business or income-producing activity (such as rental property).
- The property has a determinable useful life.
- The property is expected to last more than one year.

To claim depreciation, you must usually be the owner of the property. You are considered the owner of the property even if it's subject to a debt.

Generally if you pay rent for the property, you can't depreciate that property. Usually only the owner can depreciate it. However, if you make permanent improvements to leased property, you may be able to depreciate the improvements.

You begin to depreciate your rental property when you place it in service for the production of income.

You stop depreciating it either when you have fully recovered your cost or other basis, or when you retire it from service, whichever happens first.

The basis of the property you buy is usually its cost. The cost is the amount you pay for it in cash or in debt obligation. If you buy real property, such as a building and land, certain fees and other expenses you pay are part of the cost basis of the property.

The following settlement fees and closing costs for buying the property are part of the basis of the property.

- Abstract fees.
- Legal fees.
- Recording fees.
- Surveys
- Transfer taxes.
- Title Insurance.

So let's look at the recovery period for rental property. As covered in an earlier chapter, it is important to breakdown the purchase price of the investment property into four parts to determine the number of years to depreciate.

Residential Rental Building	27.5 years
Land Improvements	15.0 years
Personal Property	5.0 years
Land	0.0 years

The value of the land cannot be depreciated. Land Improvements would include roads, driveways, landscaping, fences. Personal property would include appliances, carpeting and furniture used in the residential rental.

The IRS defines residential real estate as a rental with at least a month to month lease. If you rent the property by the day, week or any time less than a month, it is considered a commercial property and would be depreciated over 39 years.

Chapter 18

Reporting Income, Expenses and Losses

The basic form for reporting residential rental income and expenses is Schedule E. However, don't use that schedule to report a not-for-profit activity.

If you rent homes, rooms, or apartments and provide basic services such as heat and light, trash collection, etc., you would report your rental income and expenses on Schedule E, Part 1.

List your total income, expenses and depreciation for each rental property. Be sure to enter the number of fair rental and personal use days on line 2. If you own more than three rental properties, complete and attach as many Schedules E as are needed to separately list all of the properties. However, fill in lines 23a through 26 on only one Schedule E. The figures on lines 23a through 26 on that Schedule E should be the combined totals for all properties reported on your Schedule E.

Real Estate As An Investment

[Schedule E (Form 1040 or 1040-SR), Supplemental Income and Loss, 2019 — IRS tax form]

Tom Whitehouse

At this point we need to discuss losses. One of the benefits of real estate investments, as covered in earlier chapters, is that depreciation usually creates a loss even when the property has a positive cash flow.

Generally speaking, rental real estate activities are passive activities. For this purpose, a rental activity is an activity from which you receive income mainly for the use of tangible property, rather than for services. In this case losses can only be used to offset other passive income. The IRS classifies income as follows.

Three Types of Income

ACTIVE
Job
Commission
Wages
Salary

PORTFOLIO
Interest
Dividends

PASSIVE
Limited Partnerships
Sale of Stock
Rental Real Estate

If you or your spouse actively participated in a passive rental real estate activity, you may be able to deduct your losses, with certain restrictions, against your nonpassive income. You actively participated in a rental real estate activity if you and your spouse owned at least 10% of the rental property and you made management decisions or arranged for others to provide services, such as repairs, in a significant sense.

Here are the rules and restrictions.

Before 1986, there were no restrictions on losses that could be written off against nonpassive income and wealthy investors were using real estate to eliminate paying taxes on their Active income. For that reason the federal government passed what is known as the Tax Simplification Act of 1986.

In this Act, Passive losses against Active Income was capped at $25,000 for tax payers whose Adjusted Gross Income was less than $100,000. For every $2 above $100,000 you lose $1 of loss deduction which means when your Adjusted Gross Income reaches $150,000 you cannot write off the losses. You don't lose them, they can be carried forward to a year that you would qualify for the deduction.

Then in 1994 there were changes to the Act. The new rules stated that if half of your work time is self-employed in a "real estate related" business and that half was equal to or greater than 750 hours per year, then your losses from real estate investments would not be subject to the $25,000 limit or the $100,000 phase out. You can write off all of your losses against your Active income. Only one spouse has to meet the rule and the entire family qualifies.

So, if a non-working spouse spent 750 hours per year which is 14.5 hours per week working in a real estate related business, the family filing a joint return could write off losses against the working spouses income.

In order to qualify as working in a real estate related business you would perform any of the following tasks regarding your real estate investments:

- Develops or Redevelops it.

- Constructs or Reconstructs it.

- Acquires it.

- Converts it.

- Rents or Leases it.
- Operates or Manages it.

Special Situations.

There is also a special situation where you can deduct expenses if you rent part of your property. You can deduct the expenses related to the part of the property used for rental purposes, such as home mortgage interest, mortgage insurance and real estate taxes as rental expenses on Schedule E. You can also deduct as rental expenses, a portion of other expenses that are normally nondeductible personal expenses such as electricity or painting the outside of the house. You don't have to divide the expenses that belong only to the rental part of the property but you would divide the other expenses. The best method is using the square feet. Take the percentage of the rental portion and apply it to all expenses. For example, if the area you rent is 200 square feet and your entire home is 2000 square feet, you can deduct 10% of household expenses as rental expenses.

PART SIX

YOUR IRA CAN OWN REAL ESTATE

Tom Whitehouse

Chapter 19

Self-Directed IRA

Like a traditional IRA account, a self-directed IRA (SDIRA) allows owners to defer taxes until retirement age, regardless of the level of returns. However, there are many rules and regulations that real estate investors and account owners must follow in order to receive all of these potential benefits. These rules will be reviewed in the next chapter.

Using your SDIRA to invest in alternative assets, such as real estate, will require you to follow important rules and processes. The benefits of using a SDIRA to invest in income property, include (1) increased ROI potential, (2) the ability to take control of your financial future, and (3) protect yourself against economic fluctuations.

Increased ROI Potential.

The SDIRA gives you the freedom that you need to invest in alternative assets. This means that you will have an increased level of flexibility regarding the amount of risk that you want to incur, as well as the potential for a higher ROI.

Take Control of Your Financial Future.

As the name suggests, a self-directed IRA puts you in charge of your own financial future. With the help of a real estate IRA and trusted accountant, you can make the right financial decisions for your retirement needs and goals.

Protect Against Economic Fluctuations.

The stock market can be volatile which is why diversification is key to protecting your wealth. The ability to invest in alternative assets, such as real estate, can help you to create a healthy level of diversification, while simultaneously capitalizing on investment opportunities.

To put these benefits into perspective, imagine that you purchase a home for $100,000 and sell it for $200,000. If this property was owned by your

SDIRA, then all of the profit would go back into your IRA and subsequently be tax deferred.

Now imagine that you own a home and rent it annually to a tenant for $40,000. If the property was owned by your self-directed IRA, once again, your rental income would go back into the IRA and thus be tax deferred. So it is very simple: with the help of an SDIRA you can increase your wealth, while enjoying the benefits of tax deferment.

You will eventually have to pay taxes on the tax-deferred income in your IRA when you take the cash out. For this reason, many investors choose a self-directed Roth IRA, which is similar to a traditional IRA, except for the way it handles taxes. With the Roth IRA, you actually pay your taxes before placing those funds in the Roth account. Any profit made within the Roth can be taken out tax free when you retire.

A self-directed IRA can be complicated, which is why it is important to have a real estate IRA custodian to help guide you. A custodian will help you understand the IRS code, to ensure that you are following established guidelines to avoid penalties and receive the numerous benefits.

If you plan on using a self-directed IRA to purchase investment rental real estate, you must be able to generate a sufficient cash flow to cover any maintenance or repair costs.

Just because the IRS permits the use of self-directed IRAs to invest in real estate doesn't mean it is the best option for your retirement savings. There are some risks you should be aware of before you start investing, (1) not performing your due diligence, (2) fraud, (3) lack of diversification.

Not Performing Your Due Diligence.

One of the biggest mistakes you can make when purchasing investment property is not doing your due diligence. Since you are the IRA owner and the property owner, it is your responsibility to complete due diligence. From researching the current real estate market trends to analyzing the likelihood for future growth and increases in property value, it is your responsibility to ensure that the investment is sound. With this in mind, you'll want to seek the help of a trusted real estate professional to help make the right investment decisions.

Fraud.

Another risk you need to be aware of and avoid is fraud. According to the Securities and Exchange Commission (SEC), there is an increase in criminals attempting to commit fraud against self-directed IRA account holders. The large amount of money that is typically held in SDIRAs is what makes them so attractive to fraud prompters. These individuals might attempt to engage you in a "Ponzi scheme" or other fraudulent conduct. Avoiding these types of frauds is made easier when you implement the following safeguards:

- Be sure to verify that all information within each SDIRA statement.

- Do not take unsolicited investment offers.

- Ask questions and be wary if someone balks at your questions.

- "Guaranteed returns" are often too good to be true.

- When in doubt, ask a professional for help.

Lack of Diversification.

One of the final risks that you will want to address is a lack of real estate diversification. Just as it is often a poor strategy to own only one stock, it can be a poor investment strategy to own multiple versions of the same type of real estate. By only focusing on the upside potential, you may open yourself to a major risk.

And finally, you need to consider liquidity when making real estate investments with your SDIRA. This means that you might not be able to access the value of your investments when they are needed.

Chapter 20

Rules For IRA Investment

As I mentioned earlier, there are many benefits associated with using a self-directed IRA to buy real estate. The best way to experience these benefits is to follow the rules. The most important of these SDIRA rules are as follows:

1) Your IRA is not allowed to purchase property that is owned by you or a "disqualified person."

2) You cannot have indirect benefits from property that is owned by your self-directed IRA. These "indirect benefits" might include: renting the garage apartment in a house that your IRA owns.

3) IRA investments are uniquely titled, which means that you and your IRA are considered to be two separate entities; as such, investments should be titled in the name of your IRA.

4) You can purchase real estate in your SDIRA in combination with other funds. Partnerships and undivided interest are two alternatives that exist.

5) Any IRA investments that use financing are required to pay Unrelated Business Income Tax (UBIT).

6) Any expenses that are related to IRA-owned properties must be paid from the IRA. These expenses might include: building association fees, utility bills, maintenance fees, renovations, and property taxes.

7) As stated earlier, any income generated from self-directed IRA owned real estate must be returned to the IRA. In fact, any and all income that is generated by property owned within your SDIRA is required to be paid directly into your IRA.

Taxes are one of the biggest benefits of a self-directed IRA; however, they are also one of the potential pitfalls. If you don't follow all of the associated rules and regulations, you will disqualify the SDIRA and subsequently create a taxable event. Additionally, an IRA-owned real estate investment property can lose tax benefits if the property begins to operate at a loss. For example, you cannot claim depreciation on an IRA-owned real estate property.

Keep in mind that IRAs cannot be used to purchase homes that will directly benefit you, such as primary or secondary residence. Self-dealing and personal transactions are not allowed. Also, you cannot use your SDIRA to buy or sell property on behalf of a family member, unless of course you want to create a taxable event.

Finally, it is important to note that when you become 70.5 years old, you are required to begin taking minimum distributions from your IRA. Since it is hard to sell real estate holdings in small portions, you must ensure you have enough cash in your IRA accounts to cover these required distributions. If you do not have enough cash, or cannot sell your real estate holdings in small portions, you may encounter tax issues.

Starting down the road to a self-directed IRA real estate investment is much easier if you follow these five steps:

1) It is important that you consult with your accountant or financial advisor before you make any investment decisions. These individuals will help make sure that you have done your "homework" by performing thorough due diligence on the alternative assets.

2) Before you can initiate an investment, you will need to complete a Direction of Investment (DOI) form. This form contains details about the investment, such as: how much to invest, where to send the funds, and what documents need to be signed. Remember, as part of the definition for a SDIRA, the account owner directs the account trustee to make a broader range of investments.

3) Your account trustee will ensure that your chosen investment is processed per the instructions detailed in the DOI. Once the purchase is completed and the closing

finalized, your IRA will be the title owner of the acquired asset.

4) Remember that all expenses related to your IRA-owned investment must be paid from the IRA. Additionally, all income and or profits that are generated must be directly returned to the IRA.

5) The direction and lifecycle of your SDIRA is in your hands. So, if you plan on selling or leasing an asset, it is up to you; however, your appointed trustee will process the sale or lease, based on your instructions. In the event of a sale, the asset will be removed from your SDIRA and replaced with the proceeds that the sale generated.

A SDIRA can be quite complicated, especially when it comes to the taxes, which is why it is important to work with your CPA. The rules and regulations of a SDIRA must be carefully followed so that a taxable event doesn't occur. The risks associated with the SDIRA can best be avoided through a mindful approach to investment. The benefits of a SDIRA include the ability to increase the potential for growth, taking control of your financial future, and enhancing your ability to protect against economic fluctuations.

Keep in mind that tax laws can change in the blink of an eye, which is why it is always a good idea to check with your tax professional to make sure these benefits are still applicable.

If a self-directed IRA is the right retirement account for you, then you should work with your team to begin the journey towards a diversified portfolio that can result in cost savings, tax benefits, and increased wealth.

Some Final Thoughts

As I mentioned earlier, I wrote this book with two goals in mind. One was to share my experience with real estate investing, and to provide you a system to help you set goals, learn to evaluate investment opportunities and create a successful strategy. The second goal was to assist you when you are working with investor clients or any clients that might be interested in learning more about real estate as an investment.

This entire book is about building wealth. In terms of creating financial wealth, one of the best ways I've seen, that is truly accessible to anyone, is to invest in real estate. Real estate investing can be the best avenue to wealth. It can and will change your life and your family's future.

For this to be true you need to agree with two important thoughts:

1) Building financial wealth through real estate is possible.

2) Building financial wealth through real estate is possible for you.

History has proven the first point, I'm sure you know that investing in real estate has made many others very wealthy. But, you must also believe the second point, that you really believe that it's possible for you. Many people can't get their minds around the idea that they too can attain real financial wealth through investing. So, get your mind in the right place and take action.

To achieve the second goal, working with investor clients, I would strongly encourage you to take the benefits, potential ROI and strategy for investing and create what I call your "fifteen minute" presentation. You'll be surprised at how often you will find people who never really considered real estate investing that will want to know more about the process.

I'd like to share one more story that I experienced several years ago that might be useful to you, your family, friends or some of your clients.

I got a call one day from a gentleman named David from New York. I was working in Michigan at the time and he explained to me that his son and one of his friends, who is from Michigan, were planning to go to college in my area. He wanted me to find them a place to rent near campus, they didn't want to live on campus but wanted to be close by. I told him I would take a look and get back to him.

During my conversation with David, I learned that he was an executive at a large company and had financial resources. So, I called him the next day and told him I had found a place. He said great, how much is the rent. I then told him that it wasn't for rent, it was for sale. He was a little angry and reminded me that he simply wanted to find a place for his son to rent. I said, let me explain. This is a two story house, two blocks from campus. It has four bedrooms and another bed in a room downstairs. This would accommodate his son, friend and three other students. I told him the going rate for campus rentals was $400 per bed per month. That means he would have a monthly income of

$1600 and the really good news is that the property was listed for $96,000. He said this was a lot to take in so he would have to get back to me.

Two hours later he called and said, let's do it. I told him, there's more good news; your son will be the property manager, collecting rent, calling when they need a plumber and that the going rate for campus property management is 20% of gross rent. That means he can give his son $320 per month and it's tax deductible. I helped him acquire the property, within two weeks I had all beds full of students and this continued for four years.

I continued to stay in touch with David during this time and always encouraged him to invest in real estate in his area. Four years later his son graduated, he sent me a nice card announcing his graduation. One day he called and said I think we should sell the house. I put it on the market and had it sold in a few weeks. During this time, the property values in the area had risen substantially. After we closed David called me and he seemed very pleased. He said, four years ago I called you and ask you to find a rental for my son, you talked me into buying a house and now I have sold it and the profit I made covered the entire four year tuition. My son basically went to school for free as a result of your advice. He also told me that I would be happy to know that he had purchased three investment properties in his area.

The results won't always be the same as David's but this strategy has become very popular in college towns. I've told this story in my class and several agents have reported to me that they have helped others make this type of investment for their kids.

Tom Whitehouse

ACKNOWLEDGEMENTS

In Part Four, 1031 Exchange, I would like to acknowledge the company IPX1031 Exchange Services and thank them for the information that they have shared with me. They are a national company that specializes in 1031 exchange transactions. I have worked with them and they do an amazing job.

Much of the information in Part Five can be found at IRS.org. Tax laws can and do change often so always check with your CPA or Tax Professional to get an update on the laws.

Tom Whitehouse

ABOUT THE AUTHOR

Tom Whitehouse has a Bachelors Degree in Business Administration and worked 18 years in Corporate Finance, serving as the CFO and Treasure of a $350 million company. He has been a Real Estate Broker since 1994. His Real Estate Designations include, CRB (Certified Real Estate Brokerage Manager), CRS (Certified Residential Specialist), and GRI (Graduate REALTOR Institute). He served as the President of his local Board of REALTORS, Director of his State Association and served on committees at the National Association of REALTORS. Tom holds seminars on Geographic Farming and Real Estate Investing.

Tom Whitehouse

[